SILVER·BURDETT

Making Music

Keyboard Accompaniments

Teacher's Edition Part Two
Grade 4

PEARSON

Scott
Foresman

Editorial Offices: Glenview, Illinois • Parsippany, New Jersey • New York, New York
Sales Offices: Needham, Massachusetts • Duluth, Georgia • Glenview, Illinois
Coppell, Texas • Sacramento, California • Mesa, Arizona

ISBN: 0-328-07774-7

Contents

To the Teacher

Keyboard accompaniments are provided for those songs for which the keyboard is an appropriate instrument or a reasonable substitute for authentic instruments.

The purpose of this book is to provide accompaniments for all levels of playing abilities. The chord symbols have been reproduced from the Teacher and/or Student edition and can be used by keyboard players looking for the most basic accompaniment, or for chording with instruments such as Autoharp and guitar. Harmonies in an accompaniment may differ from those on the recording and from the indicated chord symbols.

For a more elaborate treatment of instrumentation and harmonization, refer to the corresponding song recordings in the MAKING MUSIC CD package. While all of the keyboard accompaniments are in the same key as the recorded versions of the songs, occasional modulations may occur in the recordings.

The triangle-shaped indicators within an accompaniment designate the beginnings of lines of music on the student page.

Turn the Beat Around

Words and Music by Peter Jackson Jr., and Gerald Jackson
Arranged by Buddy Skipper

4

Love to hear__ per - cus - sion.

Turn it up - side down.____ Love to hear__ per - cus -

sion. Love to hear__ it. Blow, horns, you sure sound pret -

ty. Your vi - o - lins keep mov - in' to the nit - ty grit -

ty. When you hear the scratch of the gui - tar scratch -

ing, then you know that rhy - thm cor - ners all the ac -

tion, whoa___ yeah. Turn the beat___ a - round.___

Love to hear___ per - cus - sion. Turn it up - side down,___

Put a Little Love in Your Heart

Words and Music by Jimmy Holiday,
Randy Myers, and Jackie De Shannon
Arranged by Buddy Skipper

Soldier, Soldier

Traditional Song from the United States and England
Arranged by Anita P. Davis

2. . . . hat . . . hatter

3. . . . . coat . . . tailor

Haul Away, Joe

Sea Shantey from England
Arranged by Buddy Skipper

2. Oh, once I was in Ireland diggin' turf and 'taties, . . .
   But now I'm on a lime-juice ship hauling on the braces, . . .

3. King Louie was the King of France before the revolution, . . .
   King Louie got his head cut off which spoiled his constitution, . . .

Gakavik *(The Partridge)*

English Words by Mary Shamrock

Folk Song from Armenia
Arranged by Alice Firgau

Si - rov____ nig, si - rov - nig,
Soar____ and____ sail, she's fly - ing far__ and free.

si - rov - nig,____ nakh - shoun ga - ka - vik.
Pret - ty par - tridge, love - ly bird, greet - ing you and me.

Limbo Like Me

Words and Music adapted by Massie Patterson and Sammy Heyward
Arranged by Audre F. Morrison

"Limbo Like Me" New words and new music adapted by Massie Patterson and Sammy Heyward. (Based on a traditional song) TRO-© 1963 (Renewed) Ludlow Music, Inc., New York, NY. Used by permission.

Gonna Ride Up in the Chariot

African American Spiritual
Arranged by W. R. Colbrook

2. Gonna meet my brother there, yes, Soon-a in the mornin',
   Meet my brother there, yes, Soon-a in the mornin',
   Meet my brother there, yes, Soon-a in the mornin',
   And I hope I'll join the band. *Refrain*

3. Gonna chatter with the angels, Soon-a in the mornin',
   Chatter with the angels, Soon-a in the mornin',
   Chatter with the angels, Soon-a in the mornin',
   And I hope I'll join the band. *Refrain*

17

Deep in the Heart of Texas

Words by June Hershey

Music by Don Swander
Arranged by Joyce Kalbach

Tsuki   (The Moon)

English Words by Kazuo Akiyama

School Song from Japan
Arranged by Carol Jay

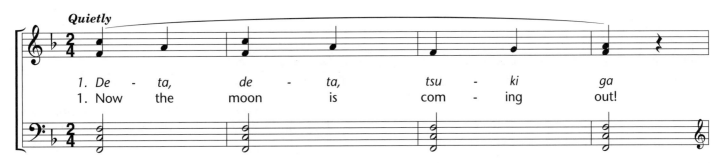

1. De - ta,   de - ta,   tsu - ki   ga
1. Now   the   moon   is   com - ing   out!

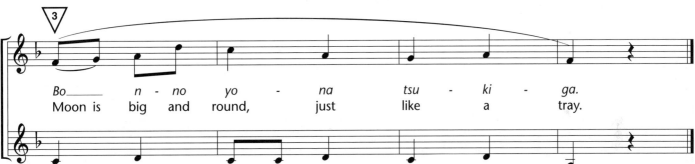

Ma - ru - i   ma - ru - i   ma - n   ma - ru - i,
Big   and   round,   so   big   and   round,   as   round___   as   a   tray.

Bo___   n - no   yo - na   tsu - ki - ga.
Moon   is   big   and   round,   just   like   a   tray.

2. *Kaku reta kumoni,*
   Kuroi, kuroi makuroi,
   Sumino yona kumoni.

2. Now the moon is hiding,
   Gone away, O gone away, O gone away so far.
   Up behind the clouds as black as tar.

Waitin' for the Light to Shine *from BIG RIVER*

Words and Music by Roger Miller
Arranged by John Girt

I have lived in the dark-ness for so long, I am wait-in' for the light to

shine.

wait-in' for the light, I am wait-in' for the light, I am

wait - in' for the light to shine.

I'm Gonna Sing The accompaniment for this
song is found on p. 26.

Sonando

English Words by Alice Firgau

Words and Music by Peter Terrace
Arranged by Ted Solis, Adapted and Arranged by Kay Edwards
Piano Arrangement by Alice Firgau

So - nan - do (clap) pa - ra bai - lar, Go - za (clap) Come on,
They're play - ing a cha-cha-cha.

mi cha - cha - cha
let's have some fun.

Lle - ga - ré Ma - rí - a, lle - ga - ré.
Here I am, Ma - rí - a, dance with me.

Tie Me Kangaroo Down, Sport

Words and Music by Rolf and Bruce Harris
Arranged by Buddy Skipper

3. Take me koala back, Jack.
   Take me koala back.
   He lives somewhere on the track, Mac.
   So take me koala back.
   All together now! *Refrain*

4. Mind me platypus duck, Bill.
   Mind me platypus duck.
   Don't let him go running amok, Bill.
   So mind me platypus duck.
   All together now! *Refrain*

5. Play your didgeridoo, Blue.
   Play your didgeridoo.
   Keep playing 'til I shoot thro', Blue.
   Play your didgeridoo.
   All together now! *Refrain*

6. Tan me hide when I'm dead, Fred.
   Tan me hide when I'm dead.
   So we tanned his hide when he died, Clyde.
   And that's it hanging on the shed.
   All together now! *Refrain*

I'm Gonna Sing

African American Spiritual
Arranged by Carmino Ravosa

2. I'm gonna shout when the spirit says "Shout," *(3 times)*
   And obey the spirit of the Lord.

3. I'm gonna pray when the spirit says "Pray," *(3 times)*
   And obey the spirit of the Lord.

4. I'm gonna sing when the spirit says "Sing," *(3 times)*
   And obey the spirit of the Lord.

Pay Me My Money Down

Work Song from the Georgia Sea Islands
Collected and Adapted by Lydia A. Parrish
Arranged by Francis Girard

Brightly

1. I thought I heard the cap-tain say, "Pay me my
2. As soon as the boat was clear of the bar, "Pay me my

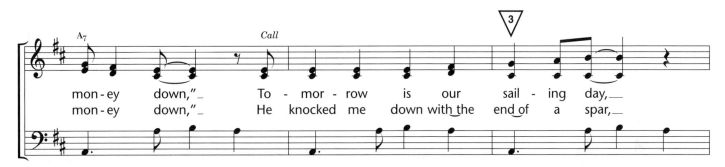

mon-ey down," To-mor-row is our sail-ing day,
mon-ey down," He knocked me down with the end of a spar,

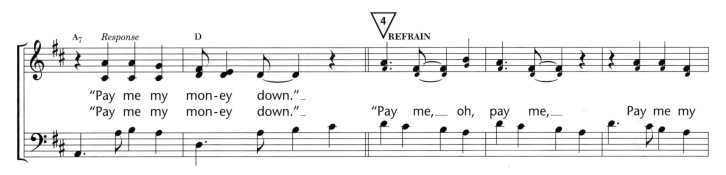

"Pay me my mon-ey down." "Pay me, oh, pay me, Pay me my
"Pay me my mon-ey down."

mon-ey down. Pay me or go to jail, Pay me my mon-ey down."

3. Well, I wish I was Mr. Steven's son,
"Pay me my money down,"
Sit on the bank and watch the work done,
"Pay me my money down."   *Refrain*

We Go Together

Lyrics and Music by Warren Casey and Jim Jacobs
Arranged by Buddy Skipper

1. We go to - geth - er,___ like ra - ma la - ma la - ma ka
2. We're one of a kind___ like dip da dip da dip

ding - a da ding___ a - dong, Re - mem - bered for -
doo - wop___ da doo - bee doo. Our names___ are

wha - oooh,   yeah!

one,_____ wa wa_ wa waah._____

When we   go out at night,_   and stars   are shin - in' bright_

Sha na na na na na na na ding-a da ding - a dong Wop ba - ba loo-bop, a -

wop bam boom We're for each oth - er___ like

wop ba - ba loo-bop, a - wop bam boom.___ Just like my broth - er___ is

sha - na - na - na - na - na - yip - pi - ty dip___ de doom. Chang chang

chang - it - ty chang___ shoo - bop, we'll al - ways be_____ to -

geth - er,_____ wha - oooh,

yeah! We'll al - ways_____ be to - geth - er._____

_____ We'll al - ways_____ be to - geth - er._____

_____ Wop ba - ba, loo - bop, a - wop bam boom!

Oh, Danny Boy

Words by Thomas Moore

Folk Melody from Ireland
Arranged by Buddy Skipper

1. Oh, Dan - ny Boy, the pipes, the pipes are call - ing, From glen to
2. But when you come and all the flow'rs are dy - ing, If I am

glen, and down the moun-tain-side; The sum-mer's gone, and all the ro - ses
dead, as dead I well may be; You'll come and find the place where I am

fall - ing, 'Tis you, 'tis you must go, and I must bide. But come ye
ly - ing, And kneel and say an A - ve there for me. And I shall

back when sum-mer's in the mead - ow, Or when the val - ley's hushed and white with
hear, tho' soft you tread a - bove me, And all my grave will war - mer, sweet - er

snow, 'Tis I'll be here in sun-shine or in sha - dow, Oh, Dan-ny
be, For you will bend and tell me that you love me, And I shall

Boy, oh, Dan - ny Boy, I love you so.
sleep in peace un - til you come to me.

Student Page 53

Somebody's Knockin' at Your Door

African American Spiritual
Arranged by Elsie Plant

With feeling

Some - bod - y's knock-in' at your door, Some - bod - y's knock-in' at your door.

Oh,_____ sin - ner, why don't you an - swer? Some - bod - y's knock-in' at your door.

Rock Island Line

Edited with New Additional Material by Alan Lomax

Railroad Song
New Words and Arrangement by Huddie Ledbetter
Arranged by Bill Wallace

Vigorously
REFRAIN

I say the Rock Is - land Line is a might - y good road, I say the

Rock Is - land Line is the road to ride. I say the Rock Is - land Line is a

might - y good road, If you want to ride it, got to ride it like you find it, Get your

tick - et at the sta - tion for the Rock Is - land Line. *Fine* VERSE

1. May be right and I
2. A, B, C, dou - ble

D.C. al Fine

maybe wrong,— Know you're gon - na miss me_____ when I'm gone.
X, Y, Z,_____ Cats_____ in the cup - board, but they don't see me.

Joe Turner Blues

Blues Song from the United States
Arranged by Richard Shadroui

River

Words and Music by Bill Staines
Arranged by Georgette LeNorth

Hashewie (Going 'Round)

Words by Hidaat Ephrem

Folk Song from Eritrea, Africa
Arranged by Carol Jay

With a strong rhythm

Call
Ha - shew - i - e_____
I will go 'round,_

Response
Shew - i - e
Shew - i - e

Call
Ha - shew - i - e_____
You will go 'round,

[2]
Response
___ Shew - i - e
Shew - i - e

Call
Ha - shew - i - e_____
We all go 'round,_

Response
Shew - i - e
Shew - i - e

Fine

[3]
Call (Tigrinya)
Bi - ha - de ha - bir - na
Ha-shew - ie e - na - bel - na
A - lem kit - fel - to
Ku - lu - me - nin - et - na
Ha-shew - i - e ni - bel
Nef' - lit - a - di - na
Bi - ha - de ha - bir - na

Response
Shew - i - e.

D.C. al Fine

Call (English)
All to - geth - er 'round,
Say - ing 'round and 'round,
So the world would know,
Who___ we___ are,
Let's___ say___ 'round,
All to - geth - er 'round,
Go - ing 'round and 'round,

Response
Shew - i - e.

43

Riqui rán

Translated by J. Olcutt Sanders

Folk Song from Latin America
Arranged by Carol Jay

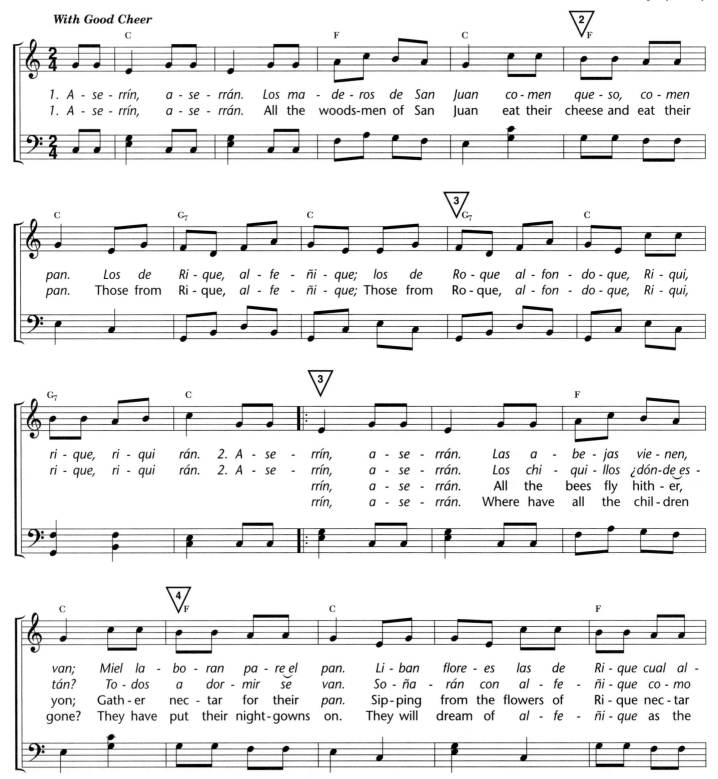

With Good Cheer

1. A - se - rrín, a - se - rrán. Los ma - de - ros de San Juan co - men que - so, co - men
1. A - se - rrín, a - se - rrán. All the woods - men of San Juan eat their cheese and eat their

pan. Los de Ri - que, al - fe - ñi - que; los de Ro - que al - fon - do - que, Ri - qui,
pan. Those from Ri - que, al - fe - ñi - que; Those from Ro - que, al - fon - do - que, Ri - qui,

ri - que, ri - qui rán. 2. A - se - rrín, a - se - rrán. Las a - be - jas vie - nen,
ri - que, ri - qui rán. 2. A - se - rrín, a - se - rrán. Los chi - qui - llos ¿dón - de es -
rrín, a - se - rrán. All the bees fly hith - er,
rrín, a - se - rrán. Where have all the chil - dren

van; Miel la - bo - ran pa - re el pan. Li - ban flore - es las de Ri - que cual al -
tán? To - dos a dor - mir se van. So - ña - rán con al - fe - ñi - que co - mo
yon; Gath - er nec - tar for their pan. Sip - ping from the flowers of Ri - que nec - tar
gone? They have put their night - gowns on. They will dream of al - fe - ñi - que as the

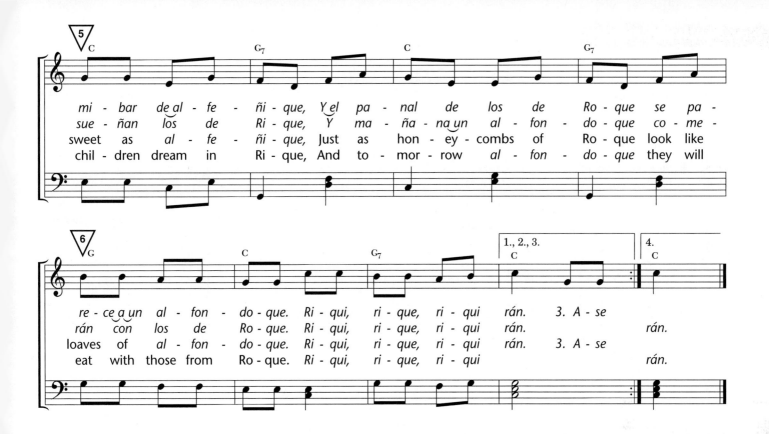

Eh, cumpari! (Hey, Buddy!)

Words and Music by Julius La Rosa and Archie Bleyer
Arranged by Buddy Skipper

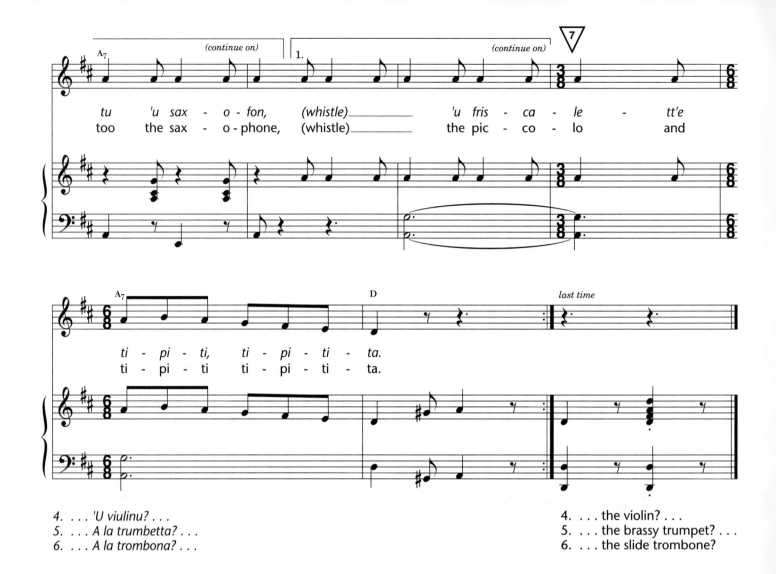

tu   'u sax - o - fon,   (whistle)_____   'u fris - ca - le - tt'e
too   the sax - o - phone, (whistle)_____   the pic - co - lo   and

ti - pi - ti,   ti - pi - ti - ta.
ti - pi - ti   ti - pi - ti - ta.

4. . . . 'U viulinu? . . .
5. . . . A la trumbetta? . . .
6. . . . A la trombona? . . .

4. . . . the violin? . . .
5. . . . the brassy trumpet? . . .
6. . . . the slide trombone?

Sourwood Mountain

Folk Song from the Appalachian Mountains
Arranged by Anita P. Davis

2. My true love's
   a blue-eyed daisy, Hey, . . .
If I don't get her
   I'll go crazy, Hey, . . .
Big dogs bark
   and little ones bite you, Hey, . . .
Big girls court
   and little ones slight you, Hey, . . .

3. My true love
   lives by the river, Hey, . . .
A few more jumps
   and I'll be with her, Hey, . . .
My true love
   lives up in the hollow, Hey, . . .
She won't come
   and I won't follow, Hey, . . .

My Home's Across the Blue Ridge Mountains

Collected by Louis Land Bascom

Folk Song from the Southern United States
Arranged by Carol Jay

The Happy Wanderer

Words by Antonia Ridge

Music by Friedrich W. Möller
Arranged by Marilyn J. Patterson

Robustly

VERSE B♭

1. I love to go a -
2. I love to wan - der
3. I wave my hat to
4. High o - ver - head, the

wan - der - ing, A - long the moun - tain track, And
by the stream That danc - es in the sun. So
all I meet, And they wave back to me. And
sky - larks wing, They nev - er rest at home, But

as I go I love to sing, My knap - sack on my back.
joy - ous - ly it calls to me, "Come! join my hap - py song!"
black - birds call so loud and sweet From ev - 'ry green - wood tree.
just like me, they love to sing, As o'er the world we roam.

Val - de ri (val-de ri) val-de ra, (val-de ra) val-de ri, (val-de ri) val-de ra, ha, ha, ha, ha, ha, Val - de

ri, (val-de ri) val-de ra, (val-de ra)
My knap - sack on my back.
"Come! join my hap - py song!"
From ev - 'ry green - wood tree.
As o'er the world we roam.

Canoe Song

Words and Music by Margaret E. McGhee
Arranged by Rene LeCLair

Brightly

Dm

1. My pad - dle's keen and bright, Flash - ing with sil - ver,
2. Dip, dip and swing her back, Flash - ing with sil - ver,

2 Dm

Fol - low the wild goose flight, Dip, dip and swing.
Fol - low the wild goose track, Dip, dip and swing.

Hey, m'tswala

Folk Song from Africa
Arranged by Christopher Hatcher

Steadily

Hey, m'tswa - la, ne - ye ti - pa ya - me tswa - la.

54

Paw-Paw Patch

Play-Party Song from the United States
Arranged by Cameron McGraw

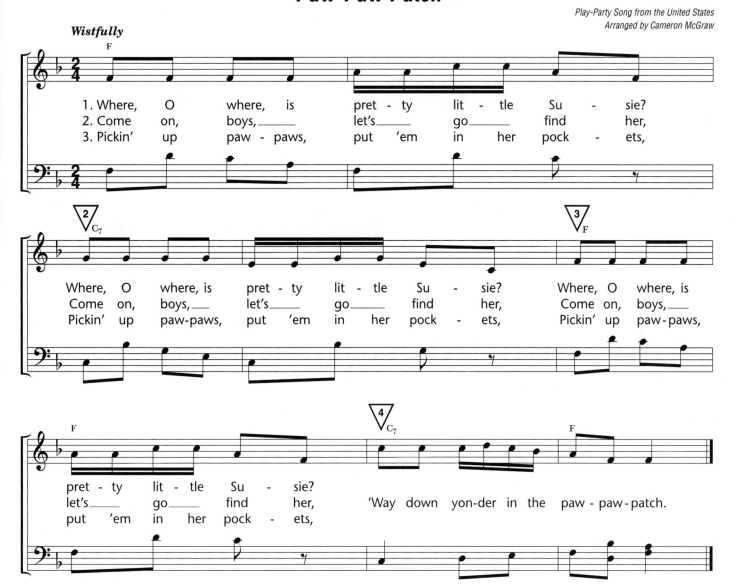

Wistfully

1. Where, O where, is pret-ty lit-tle Su-sie?
2. Come on, boys, let's go find her,
3. Pickin' up paw-paws, put 'em in her pock-ets,

Where, O where, is pret-ty lit-tle Su-sie? Where, O where, is
Come on, boys, let's go find her, Come on, boys,
Pickin' up paw-paws, put 'em in her pock-ets, Pickin' up paw-paws,

pret-ty lit-tle Su-sie?
let's go find her, 'Way down yon-der in the paw-paw-patch.
put 'em in her pock-ets,

Ōsamu kosamu *(Biting Wind)*

English Words by Gloria J. Kiester

Folk Song from Japan
Arranged by John Detroy

Walk in Jerusalem

African American Spiritual
Arranged by W. R. Colbrook

he de-clared he'd meet me there,— Walk in Je-ru-sa-lem just like John.
I'll be there in the com-ing day,— Walk in Je-ru-sa-lem just like John.

Cement Mixer

Words and Music by Slim Gaillard and Lee Ricks
Arranged by Buddy Skipper

First you get some grav - el, Pour it in a vout; To

mix a mess o' mor - tar, you add ce - ment and wa - ter.

See the mel - low roon - y come out,_____ slurp, slurp, slurp.

Who wants a buck - et of ce - ment?

Rise and Shine

Folk Song from the United States
Arranged by Marilyn J. Patterson

First time: G
Second time: B

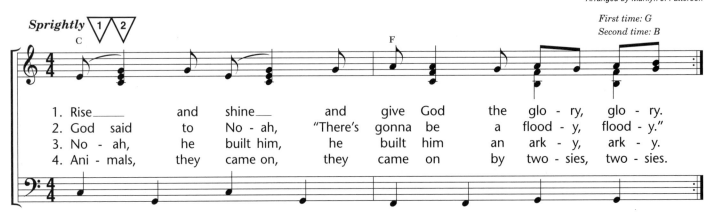

1. Rise_____ and shine_____ and give God the glo - ry, glo - ry.
2. God said to No - ah, "There's gonna be a flood - y, flood - y."
3. No - ah, he built him, he built him an ark - y, ark - y.
4. Ani - mals, they came on, they came on by two - sies, two - sies.

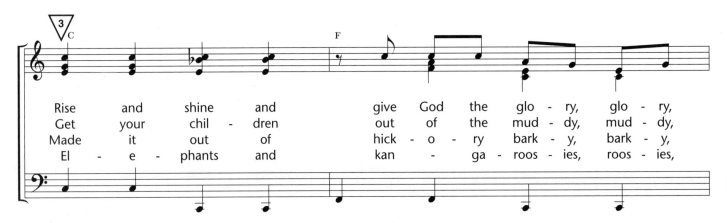

Rise and shine and give God the glo - ry, glo - ry,
Get your chil - dren out of the mud - dy, mud - dy,
Made it out of hick - o - ry bark - y, bark - y,
El - e - phants and kan - ga - roos - ies, roos - ies,

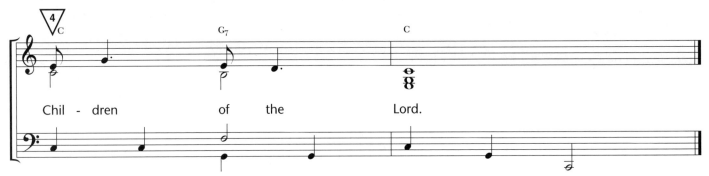

Chil - dren of the Lord.

5. Rained and rained
for forty daysies, daysies.
Rained and rained
for forty daysies, daysies.
Nearly drove those animals crazy, crazy,. . .

6. Noah, he sent out,
he sent out a dovey, dovey.
Noah, he sent out,
he sent out a dovey, dovey.
Sent him to the heavens abovey, bovey,. . .

7. Sun came out
and dried off the landy, landy.
Sun came out
and dried off the landy, landy.
Ev'rything was fine and dandy, dandy,. . .

8. This is the end,
the end of my story, story.
This is the end,
the end of my story, story.
Ev'rything is hunky-dory, dory,. . .

Weevily Wheat

Traditional
Arranged by Linda Williams

Don't want your wee-vi-ly wheat, Don't want your bar - ley,

Take some flour in half an hour and bake a cake for Char - lie.

Five times five is twen-ty-five, Five times six is thir - ty,

Five times sev'n is thir-ty five, Five times eight is for - ty.

See the Children Playin'

Words by Reginald Royal

Folk Melody from Mississippi
Arranged by Rosemary Jacques

Son macaron

Traditional
Arranged by Marilyn J. Patterson

Son ma - ca - ron, son far - ee - on. Mar - i - on,

mar - i - on, le - ya le - ya tip tip tip. Le - ya le - ya tap tap tap.

One beat, two beats, three beats, catch!

65

Turn the World Around

Words by Harry Belafonte

Music by Robert Freedman
Arranged by Marilyn J. Patterson

4. Water make the river,
   river wash the mountain,
   Fire make the sunlight,
   turn the world around.

5. Heart is of the river
   body is the mountain,
   Spirit is the sunlight,
   turn the world around.

6. We are of the spirit,
   truly can the spirit,
   Only can the spirit,
   turn the world around.

Over My Head

African American Spiritual
Arranged by Rosemary Jacques

Straighten Up and Fly Right

The accompaniment for this song is found on p. 71.

The Lion Sleeps Tonight (Wimoweh)(Mbube)

Words and Revised Music by George David Weiss, Hugo Peretti, and Luigi Creatore
Arranged by John Girt

Straighten Up and Fly Right

Words and Music by Nat King Cole and Irving Mills
Arranged by John Girt

71

T'hola, t'hola (Softly, Softly)

Folk Song from Africa
Arranged by Christopher Hatcher

Ochimbo

Words by Margaret Marks

Folk Song from Kenya
As Sung by Ruth Nthreketha
Arranged by Mark A. Miller

Ala Da´lona

English Words by Alice Firgau

Folk Song from Arabia
Arranged by Alice Firgau

Over the Rainbow

The accompaniment for this
song is found on p. 80.

Cumberland Gap

Play-Party Song from Kentucky
Arranged by Martha Hilley

2. Cumberland Gap is a mighty fine place, . . . *(3 times)*
   Three kinds of water to wash your face. *Refrain*

3. Cumberland Gap, with its cliffs and rocks, . . . *(3 times)*
   Home of the panther, bear, and fox. *Refrain*

4. Me and my wife and my wife's grandpap, . . . *(3 times)*
   We raise Cain at Cumberland Gap. *Refrain*

Student Page 144

Canción de cuna (Cradle Song)

Folk Song from Latin America
Arranged by Mark A. Miller

Tenderly

Duer - me pron - to, ni - ño mí - o, Duer - me pron - to y sin llo - rar.
Go to sleep now, go to sleep now, go to sleep now, lit - tle child.

Que es - tás en los bra - zos de tu ma - dre, que te va a can - tar.
You are in your moth - er's arms._ She will sing a lull - a - by.

Over the Rainbow

Words by E. Y. Harburg

Music by Harold Arien
Arranged by George Odam

Cantando mentiras *(Singing Tall Tales)*

English Words by Alice Firgau

Folk Song from Latin America
Arranged by Alice Firgau

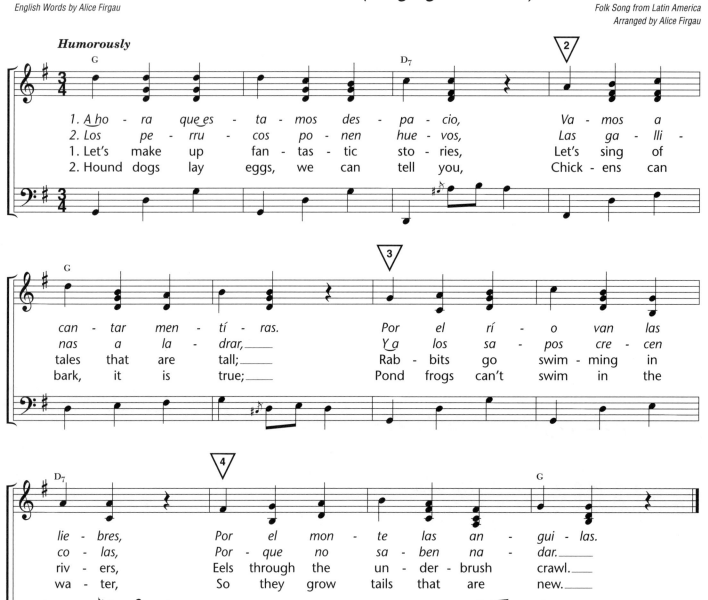

Chairs to Mend

Street Call From England
Arranged by John Courant

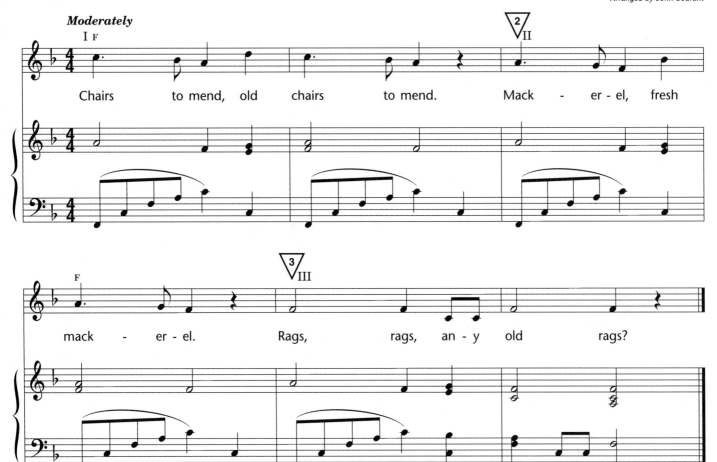

Chairs to mend, old chairs to mend. Mack - er - el, fresh

mack - er - el. Rags, rags, an - y old rags?

Ode to Joy

Words by Friedrich Schiller
English Words by Georgette LeNorth

Music by Ludwig van Beethoven
Arranged by Alan Seale and Don Kalbach

The accompaniment for this song is found on p. 86.

America, the Beautiful

Amazing Grace

Words by John Newton

Early American Melody
Arranged by Frank Fox

2. 'Twas grace that taught my heart to fear,
   And grace my fears relieved;
   How precious did that grace appear
   The hour I first believed!

3. Through many dangers, toils, and snares,
   I have already come;
   'Tis grace has brought me safe thus far,
   And grace will lead me home.

America, the Beautiful

Words by Katharine Lee Bates

Music by Samuel A. Ward
Countermelody by Buryl Red

A - mer - i - ca, the beau - ti-ful. We sing A -

shed	His	grace on thee	And crown thy good with
mend	thine	ev - 'ry flaw,	Con - firm thy soul in
shed	His	grace on thee	And crown thy good with

mer - i - ca. We sing A - mer - i - ca.

broth - er - hood	From sea to shin - ing sea!
self con - trol,	Thy lib - er - ty in law!
broth - er - hood	From sea to shin - ing sea!

Dry Bones

African American Spiritual
Arranged by George Winston

At the Hop

Words and Music by A. Singer, J. Medora, and D. White
Arranged by Buddy Skipper

2. Well, you can

Let's go to the hop!

Santa Clara

English Words by Alice Firgau

Folk Song from the Philippines
As sung by Sonny Alforque
Arranged by David Eddleman

San - ta Cla - rang, _____ pi - nung pi - no
San - ta Cla - ra, _____ this I will do.

Ang pa - nga - ko ko ay ga - ni - to.
In my heart I vow and prom - ise you,

Pag - da - ting ko po _____ sa U - ban - do.
On the road I'll go _____ to U - ban - do;

Doraji (Bluebells)

English Words by Patricia Shehan Campbell

Folk Song from Korea
Arranged by Bruce Simpson

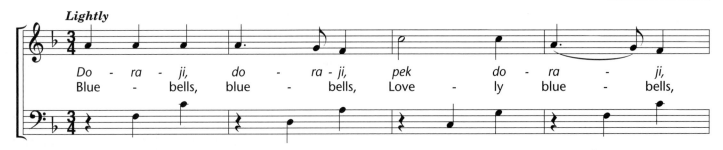

Do - ra - ji, do - ra - ji, pek do - ra - ji,
Blue - bells, blue - bells, Love - ly blue - bells,

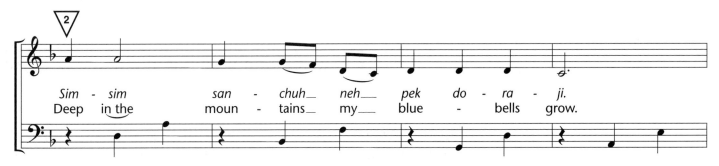

Sim - sim san - chuh neh pek do - ra - ji.
Deep in the moun - tains my blue - bells grow.

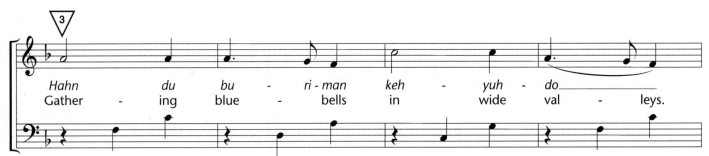

Hahn du bu - ri - man keh - yuh - do
Gather - ing blue - bells in wide val - leys.

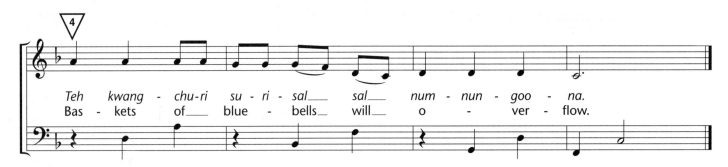

Teh kwang - chu - ri su - ri - sal sal num - nun - goo - na.
Bas - kets of blue - bells will o - ver - flow.

96

La Tarara

English Words by Alice D. Firgau

Folk Song from Spain
Arranged by Joyce Kalbach

With Feeling 𝄋 REFRAIN

La Ta - ra - ra, sí la Ta - ra - ra, no, La Ta - ra - ra,
La Ta - ra - ra, yes, La Ta - ra - ra, no, La Ta - ra - ra,

ma - dre, que la bai - lo yo.
ma - ma, is a dance I know.

VERSE

1. Tie - ne la Ta - ra - ra un jar - dín de
2. Tie - ne la Ta - ra - ra un ces - to de
1. If I want to wan - der in her gar - den
2. If I want a bas - ket of the fruit she'll

flo - res y me da, si quie - ro, siem - pre las me - jor - es. La Ta -
fru - tas y me da, si quie - ro, siem - pre las ma - du - ras. La Ta -
bow - ers, La Ta - ra - ra al - ways gives me her best flow - ers.
har - vest, La Ta - ra - ra al - ways gives me just the rip - est.

D.S. al Fine

97

Old House, Tear It Down!

Collected by John Work

African American Work Song
Arranged by John Girt

Steadily

1. Old house, tear it down! Who's gon-na help me tear it down?
2. New house, build it up! Who's gon-na help me build it up?

Bring me a ham-mer, tear it down! Bring me a saw,___ tear it down!
Bring me a ham-mer, build it up! Bring me a saw,___ build it up!

Next thing you bring me, tear it down! Is a wreck-ing ma-chine, tear it down!
Next thing you bring me, build it up! Is a car-pen-ter man, build it up!

All Night, All Day

African American Spiritual
Arranged by James Rooker

Kookaburra

Words and Music by Marion Sinclair
Arranged by William and Patrick Medley

Kook-a-bur-ra sits on the old gum tree,__ Mer-ry, mer-ry king of the bush is he.__

Laugh, kook-a-bur-ra, laugh, kook-a-bur-ra, Gay your life must be.

Missy-La, Massa-La

Game Song from the Caribbean
Arranged by Joyce Kalbach

Mis-sy-la,__ mas-sa-la,__ Mis-sy lost__ her gold ring, go 'way.

Mis-sy-la,__ mas-sa-la,__ Mis-sy lost__ her gold ring. I got to

find 'em, find 'em, find 'em, find 'em, Find 'em, let me see___ la, la, la, la

find 'em, find 'em, find 'em, find 'em, Find 'em, let me see.

Ah, Poor Bird

Traditional Round from England
Arranged by Audrey Schultz

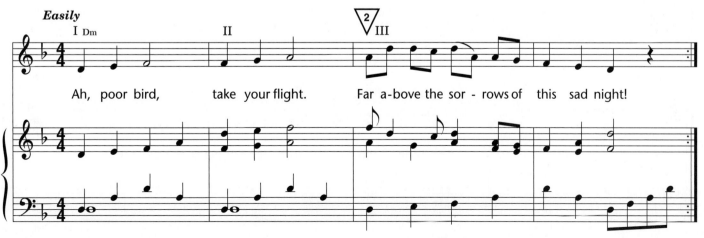

Ah, poor bird, take your flight. Far a-bove the sor - rows of this sad night!

101

Los niños en España cantan *(In Spain, the Children Sing)*

English Words by S. T.

Folk Song from Mexico
Arranged by Christopher Hatcher

Los ni - ños en Es - pa - ña can - tan, can - tan en Ja - pón, Los
In Spain, the chil - dren sing all day. Yes, al - so in Ja - pan. Oh,

pa - ja - ri - tos can - tan, can - tan to - dos su can - ción.
ev - 'ry - where the birds join in with wom - an, child, and, man.

The Computer

Words by Fitzhugh Dodson

Music by Mary Shamrock
Arranged by Joyce Kalbach

A com - put - er is a think-ing ma-chine, the smart-est one you've ev - er seen, but

ev - 'ry com-put-er can on - ly do____ what some per-son has told it to.

Frog Music

Folk Song from Canada
Arranged by Rosemary Jacques

Do Wah Diddy Diddy

Words and Music by Jeff Barry and Ellie Greenwich
Arranged by Phil Perkins

stayed a lit - tle more, Sing-in' Do wah did - dy did-dy down did-dy do.

America

Words and Music by Neil Diamond
Arranged by Buddy Skipper

Far, we've been trav - el - ing far,____

with - out____ a home,____ but not with-out a star.____

105

Free,   on - ly want__ to be free,__

we hud - dle close,__

hang on__ to a dream.__

On the boats and on   the planes,
Nev - er look - ing back   a - gain,

they're com - ing to A - mer - i - ca.
they're com - ing to A - mer - i - ca.

Home   don't it seem so   far   a - way,
Home,   to a new and a shin - y place,

oh, we're trav - el - ing light_____ to - day,
make our bed and we'll say_____ our grace,

in the eye of the storm._____
free-dom's light burn - ing warm,_____

in the eye of the storm._____
free-dom's light burn - ing warm._____

mer-i-ca.   They're com - ing to A - mer-i-ca.   They're com - ing to A -

mer-i-ca   to - day, ___   to - day, ___

to - day, ___   to - day. ___

America, the Free

Words and Music by Phyllis Wolfe-White (adapted)

112

1. I am her voice. _____ I am her voice. _____

2. I can _____ I can _____ I can _____
   (learn a lan - guage,) *(shoot a bas - ket,)* *(build the fu - ture)*

1. A - mer - i - ca!

2. proud and strong! A - mer - i - ca!

El rancho grande *(The Big Ranch)*

English Words by Alice D. Firgau

Music by Silvano R. Ramos
Arranged by William Simon

Sincerely

A - llá en el ran - cho gran - de, A - llá don - de vi -
Out yon - der on a prai - rie, The ranch where I was

ví - a, Ha - bía u - na ran - che -
liv - ing, I heard a pret - ty

ri - ta, Que a - le - gre me de - cí - a, Que a - le - gre me de - cí - a:
cow - girl, Who hap - pi - ly was sing - ing, Who hap - pi - ly was sing - ing:

REFRAIN

Te voy ha - cer tus cal -
A pair of chaps I will

zo - nes, Co - mo los u - sa el ran - che - ro;
make you, Just like the ones for a ranch-er;

Te los co - mien - zo de la - na,
With wool and leath - er I'll make them.

Te los a - ca - bo de cue - ro.
Oh, do please give me your an - swer.

Oh, How Lovely Is the Evening

Traditional German Melody
Arranged by Bruce Simpson

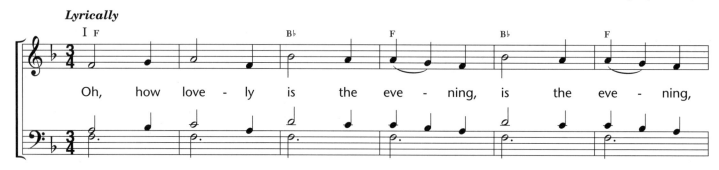

Oh, how love-ly is the eve - ning, is the eve - ning,

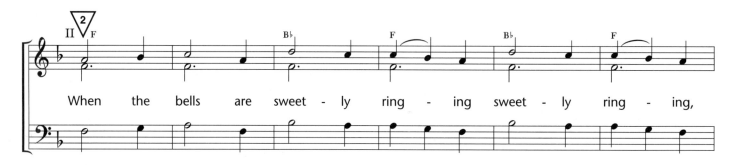

When the bells are sweet - ly ring - ing sweet - ly ring - ing,

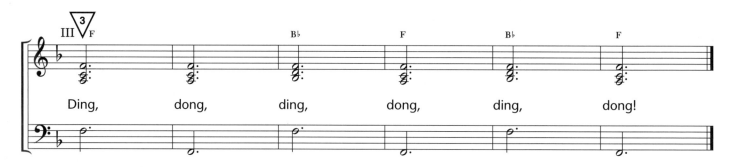

Ding, dong, ding, dong, ding, dong!

Dry Bones Come Skipping

Traditional Song from the United States
Arranged by John Girt

Lively

Dry bones come skip-ping up the val - ley. Some of them bones are mine.

Dry bones come skip-ping up the val - ley. Some of them bones are mine.

Some of them bones are 'Ze - kiel's bones. Some of them bones are mine.

Some of them bones are 'Ze - kiel's bones. Some of them bones are mine.

Minka

English Words by Margaret Marks

Folk Song from Ukraine
Arranged by Paul Beck

1. Said the Cos - sack to the maid - en, "Love, my heart is heav - y lad - en.
2. Off the Cos - sack went to bat - tle, All a - lone poor Mink - a sat E -

Du - ty calls, so I'm a - fraid, En - chant - ress, we must part._____
lev - en years, and she grew fat, Al - though her heart was true._____

I be - seech you, fair - est Mink - a, Wait for me, I hate to think An -
When at last her Cos - sack lov - er Came back home and looked her o - ver,

oth - er man might come and tink - er. With your faith - ful heart!"_____
He be - gan to court an - oth - er. Broke her heart in two!_____

Thula, thula, ngoana (Sleep, Sleep, Baby)

Folk Song from the Lesotho Region of South Africa
Arranged by Christopher Hatcher

Tenderly

Thu - la, thu - la, ngoa - na, __ thu - la, thu - la, ngoa - na, __
Sleep my lit - tle ba - by, __ sleep my lit - tle ba - by, __

Thu - la, thu - la, ngoa - na, __ thu - la, thu - la, ngoa - na. __
Sleep my lit - tle ba - by, __ sleep my lit - tle ba - by. __

121

Tengo, Tengo, Tengo (I Have Three Sheep)

English Words by Julie Scott

Folk Song from New Mexico
Arranged by E. G. McKinley

1. Ten - go, ten - go, ten - go, tú no tie - nes na - da;
2. U - na me da le - che, y o - tra me da la - na;
1. I have some - thing splen - did! And you have, you have no - thing!
2. One sheep gives me sweet milk, An - oth - er gives me wool;

Ten - go tres o - ve - jas, a - llá en la ca - ña - da.
Y o - tra man - te - qui - lla, ¡Ay! Pa - ra la se - ma - na.
I have three fine sheep, and they're graz - ing in the gul - ly.
That one gives me but - ter, Oh! it will last a week.

Tancovačka (Dancing)

Slovak Folk Song
Arranged by Robert Jameson

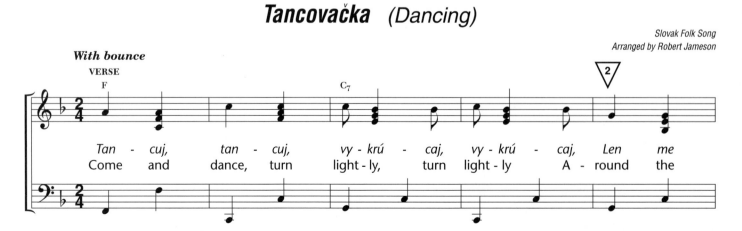

Tan - cuj, tan - cuj, vy - krú - caj, vy - krú - caj, Len me
Come and dance, turn light - ly, turn light - ly A - round the

Let Music Surround You

Words and Music by Fran Smartt Addicott
Arranged by Christopher Hatcher

Let mus-ic sur-round you, let it warm your heart.

Those who sing in har-mo-ny, nev-er___ grow a - part.

The Keel Row

Folk Song from Northumbria
Arranged by John Pivarnik

El borrego (The Lamb)

English Words by Julie Scott

Folk Song from Mexico
Arranged by Alice Firgau

Gaily

Se - ño - ra, su bo - rre - gui - to, me quie -
Se - ño - ra, your lit - tle lamb wants to take

re lle - var___ al rí - o, y yo le di - go que
me down to the cold riv - er, But I must tell the lamb,

no, por - que me mue - ro de___ frí - o.
"No!" be - cause the cold wa - ter makes___ me shiv-er.

Sweet Betsy from Pike

Folk Song from the United States
Adapted and arranged by Lillian Wiedman
Arranged by Donald Scafuri

4. The rooster ran off and the oxen all died,
   The last piece of bacon that morning was fried.
   Poor Ike got discouraged and Betsy got mad,
   The dog wagged his tail and looked awfully sad.   *Refrain*

5. The alkali desert was burning and hot,
   And Ike, he decided to leave on the spot:
   "My dear old Pike County, I'll go back to you."
   Said Betsy, "You'll go by yourself if you do."   *Refrain*

6. They swam the wide rivers, they crossed the tall peaks,
   They camped out on prairies for weeks and for weeks,
   Fought hunger and rattlers and big storms of dust,
   Determined to reach California or bust.   *Refrain*

Theme from New York, New York

Words by Fred Ebb

Music by John Kander
Arranged by John Girt

are melt-ing a - way. I'll make a brand new start_ of it

in old_ New York. If I can make it there,

I'd make it an - y-where, It's up to you, New York, New

D.S. al Coda

York. And step a -

king of the hill, head of the list, cream of the crop at the

top of the heap. My lit-tle town blues

are melt-ing a-way. I'll make a brand new start__ of it

in old New York. If I can make it there,

I'd make it an - y - where, Come on, come

through, New York, New York.

Blow, Ye Winds

Folk Song from the United States
Arranged by Benjamin Carter

3. It's now we're out to sea, my boys, the wind begins to blow,
   One half the watch is sick on deck and the other half below. *Refrain*

4. The skipper's on the quarter-deck, a-squinting at the sails,
   When up aloft the look-out sights a school of whales. *Refrain*

5. "Now clear away the boats, my boys, and after him we'll trail,
   But if you get too near to him, he'll kick you with his tail!" *Refrain*

6. Now we've got him turned up, we tow him alongside;
   We over with our blubber hooks and rob him of his hide. *Refrain*

7. Next comes the stowing down, my boys; 'twill take both night and day,
   And you'll all have fifty cents apiece when you collect your pay. *Refrain*

Rio Grande

Shantey from the United States
Arranged by Darrell Peter

3. The anchor's aweigh and the sails they are set, . . .
   The gals that we're leaving we'll never forget, . . . *Refrain*

4. Goodbye to Sally and Sarah and Sue, . . .
   To all who are list'ning, it's goodbye to you, . . . *Refrain*

'Round the Bay of Mexico

Traditional Shanty
Collected by Stan Hugill
Arranged by Ting Ho

Lustily

Solo

1. Heave a - way, my bul - ly boys,
2. Heave a - way, and a - round goes she,
3. Heave a - round and with a will,
4. Heave a - way, for she's trimmed tight,

Chorus 'Way - ay,

heave a - way!

Heave a - way, why don't you make some noise, boys?
Six for you and sev - en for me,
If she don't go she will stay there still,
Bend your backs if you want to sleep to - night,

Chorus 'Round the Bay of Mex - i - co!

How Can I Keep from Singing?

Celtic Folk Song
Arranged by Joyce Kalbach

Lyrically

1. My life flows on in end - less song, a - bove earth's lam - en - it
2. What though the tem - pest 'round me roars, I know the truth, it
3. When ty - rants trem - ble, sick with fear, And hear their death knells

The Glendy Burke

Words and Music by Stephen Foster
Arranged by Ting Ho

Oh, Susanna

Words and Music by Stephen Foster
Arranged by Albert Devito

1. I came from Al - a - ba - ma With my ban - jo on my knee, I'm
2. I had a dream the oth - er night, When ev - 'ry-thing was still, I

going to Loui - si - an - a, My true love for to see; It rained all night the
thought I saw Su-san - na A-com-ing down the hill. The buck-wheat cake was

day I left, The weath - er it was dry; The sun so hot I froze to death; Su-
in her mouth, The tear was in her eye. Says I, "I'm com-ing from the South, Su-

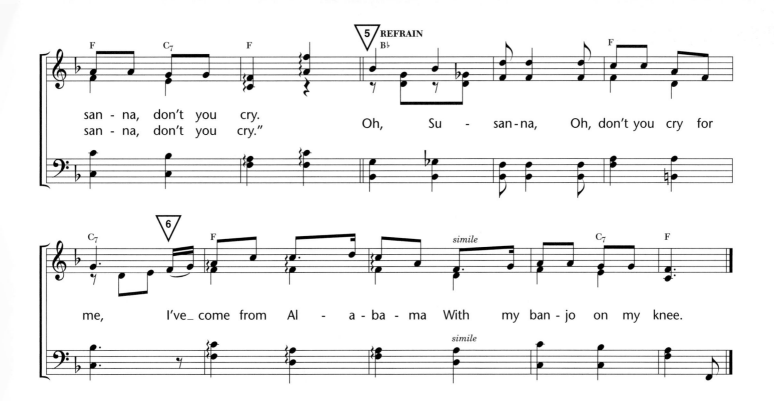

Follow the Drinkin' Gourd

Song of the Underground Railroad
Arranged by Joseph Joubert

Not too Fast
REFRAIN

Fol - low___ the drink - in' gourd.___ Fol - low___ the drink - in' gourd.___ For the

old man is a - wait-ing for to car - ry you to free-dom If you fol-low the drink - in' gourd. *Fine*

VERSE
1. When the sun comes up and the first quail calls,___ Fol - low___ the drink - in' gourd.___ For the

D.C. al Fine
old man is a - wait-ing for to car - ry you to free-dom If you fol-low the drink - in' gourd.

142

2. Now the riverbank will make a mighty good road;
Dead trees will show you the way.

And the left foot, pegfoot, travelin' on,
Just you follow the drinkin' gourd.

Wade in the Water

African American Spiritual
Arranged by Joyce Kalbach

Cielito lindo

English Words by Alice Firgau

Folk Song from Mexico
Arranged by Wallace Schmidt

1. De la sie - rra mo - re - na, Cie - li - to lin - do, vie - nen ba -
1. From the dark,___ dis - tant moun - tain, Cie - li - to lin - do, I___ see de -

jan - do,___ Un par de_o - ji - tos ne - gros, Cie - li - to
scend - ing,___ Your dark eyes___ flash - ing bright - ly, Cie - li - to

lin - do, de___ con - tra - ban - do.___ Ay, ay, ay, ay!___
lin - do, love's___ mes - sage send - ing.___ Ay, ay, ay, ay!___

Can - ta y no llo - res.___ Por - que can - tan - do se_a -
Sing, sing with glad - ness.___ For in those hearts that are

2. *Ese lunar que tienes, Cielito lindo,*
   Junto a la boca,
   No se lo des a nadie, Cielito lindo,
   que a mi me toca. Refrain

2. For your kisses, my lovely Cielito lindo,
   My heart is aching.
   And when I can't be near you, Cielito lindo,
   my heart is breaking. *Refrain*

Streets of Laredo

Cowboy Song from the United States
Arranged by Edward Paynter

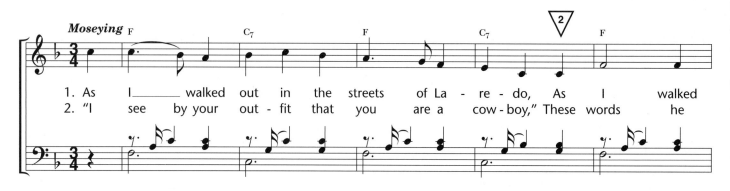

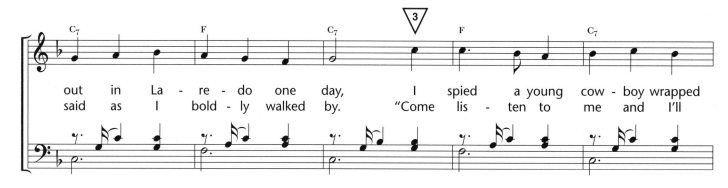

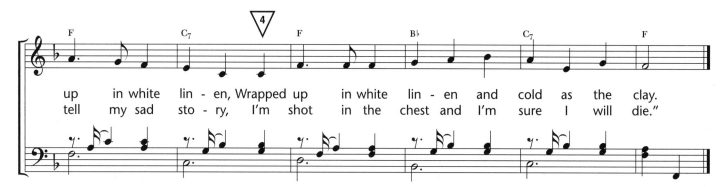

3. "Now once in the saddle I used to ride handsome,
   'A handsome young cowboy' is what they would say.
   I'd ride into town and go down to the cardhouse,
   But I'm shot in the chest and I'm dying today."

4. "Go run to the spring for a cup of cold water,
   To cool down my fever," the young cowboy said.
   But when I returned, his poor soul had departed,
   And I wept when I saw the young cowboy was dead.

5. We'll bang the drum slowly and play the fife lowly,
   We'll play the dead march as we bear him along.
   We'll go to the graveyard and lay the sod o'er him;
   He was a young cowboy, but he had done wrong.

Corrido de Kansas *(Kansas Corrido)*

English Words by David Eddleman

Folk Song from Mexico
Arranged by Carol Jay

3. *Cuando dimos vista a Kansas*
   Era puritita correr,
   Eran los camonos largos,
   Y pensaba yo en volver.

3. When we came in sight of Kansas,
   A stampede broke out a-churning,
   Down the dusty trail a-winding,
   And I thought about returning.

147

Route 66

Words and Music by Bobby Troup
Arranged by Buddy Skipper

Pastures of Plenty

Words and Music by Woody Guthrie
Arranged by Alice Firgau

1. It's a might - y hard row that my poor hands has hoed._____
2. I_____ worked in your or - chards of peach - es and prunes;_____
3. Green_____ pas - tures of plen - ty from dry de - sert ground,_____
4. It's_____ al - ways we ram - bled, that riv - er and I;_____

My poor feet has trav - eled a hot dust - y road._____
Slept on the ground__ in the light of the moon.
From the Grand Cou - lee Dam__ where the wa - ters run down.
All a - long your green val - ley I will work 'till I die._____

Out of your Dust__ Bowl and west-ward we rolled, And your
On the edge of the cit - y you'll see us and then, We_____
Ev - ery state in the Un - ion us mi - grants has been, We'll_____
My__ land I'll de - fend__ with my life if it be, 'Cause my

des - erts was hot	and your	moun - tains	was	cold.
come	with the dust	and we're	gone with	the	wind.
work	in	this fight,	and we'll	fight 'till	we	win.
pas - tures of plen - ty	must	al - ways	be	free.

California, Here I Come

Words and Music by Al Jolson, Bud DeSylva, and Joseph Meyer
Arranged by Joyce Kalbach

Cal - i - for - nia, here I come,___ Right back where I start-ed from.

Where bow - ers of flow-ers bloom in the spring.___ Each morn-ing

at dawn-ing bird - ies sing and ev - 'ry-thing. A sun - kissed miss said,

"Don't be late."___ That's why I can hard-ly wait.___ O - pen

up that Gold-en Gate.___ Cal - i - for - nia, here I come!

Cotton-Eye Joe

Folk Song from Tennessee
Arranged by Martin Quarles

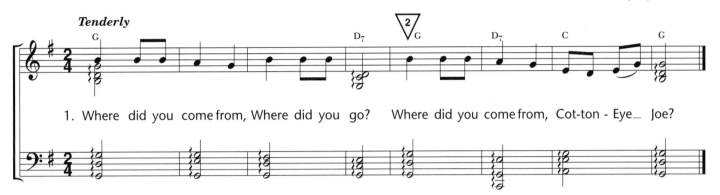

1. Where did you come from, Where did you go? Where did you come from, Cot-ton - Eye_ Joe?

2. I've come for to see you,
   I've come for to sing,
   I've come for to bring you
   A song and a ring.

3. When did you leave here?
   Where did you go?
   When you comin' back here,
   Cotton-Eye Joe?

4. Left here last winter,
   I've wandered through the year.
   Seen people dyin',
   Seen them with their fear.

5. I've been to the cities,
   Buildings cracking down,
   Seen the people calling,
   Falling to the ground.

6. I'll come back tomorrow,
   If I can find a ride,
   Or I'll sail in the breezes,
   Blowin' on the tide.

7. Well, when you do come back here,
   Look what I have brung,
   A meadow to be run in,
   A song to be sung.

8. Where did you come from?
   Where did you go?
   Where did you come from,
   Cotton-Eye Joe?

Ai, Dunaiĭ moy (Ah, My Merry Dunaii)

English Words by Charles Haywood

Folk Song from Russia
Arranged by Paul Somers

With gusto

U vo-rot, vo-rot, vo-rot Da u vo-rot ba-
At their fa-ther's gate they stand, They're gath-ered round, a

tyush-ki-mykh. Ai, Du-naiĭ moy, Du-naiĭ, Ai, ve-syo-
hap-py band. Oh, my dear Du-naii, Oh, my mer-

liy Du-naiĭ! Ra-zgu-lya-li-sya re-bya-ta, Ras-po-te-
ry Du-naii! Mer-ry lads are loud-ly sing-ing, Laugh-ing voices

shi-lis. Ai, Du-naiĭ moy, Du-naiĭ, Ai, ve-syo-liy Du-naiĭ!
hap-pi-ly ring-ing. Oh, my dear Du-naii, Oh, my mer-ry Du-naii!

156

Beriozka *(The Birch Tree)*

Folk Song from Russia
Arranged by Paul Beck

2. Oh, my little tree, I need branches,
   For three silver flutes I need three branches,
   Loo-lee-loo, three branches,
   Loo-lee-loo, three branches.

3. From another branch I will make now,
   I will make a tingling balalaika,
   Loo-lee-loo, balalaika,
   Loo-lee-loo, balalaika.

4. When I play my new balalaika,
   I will think of you, my lovely birch tree,
   Loo-lee-loo, lovely birch tree,
   Loo-lee-loo, lovely birch tree.

The Bard of Armagh

Words attributed to Thomas Campbell

Folk Tune from Ireland
Arranged by Rory Boyle

1. Oh! List to the tale of a poor Ir - ish har - per, And scorn not the
2. At wake or at fair I would twirl my shil - le - lagh, And trip through a

strings in his old with - er'd__ hand; But_ re - mem - ber those fin - gers could__
jig with my shoes bound with__ straw; And__ all the_ pret - ty maid - ens from__

once move much sharp - er, To wa - ken the ech - oes of his dear na - tive land.
vil - lage and val - ley, Love the bold Phel - im Bra - dy, the_ bard of Ar - magh.

Tina singu

Folk Song from South Africa
Arranged by Ting Ho and Don Kalbach

Ti - na sing - u le - lu - vu - tae - a Wat - sha, wat - sha, wat - sha, Ti - na,
We burn with the fire__ of life,__ oh, We burn

La raspa

English Words by Kim Williams

Folk Song from Mexico
Arranged by Joyce Kalbach

La ras - pa yo bai - lé   al de - re - cho y al re - vés.   Si
The ras - pa I will dance,   as for - ward and back I go.   So

quie - res tú bai - lar,   em - pie - za a mo - ver los pies.
if you want to dance,   be - gin with your heel and toe.

Brin - ca, brin - ca, brin - ca tam - bién,   mue - ve, mue - ve mu - cho los pies.   Que la
Al - ways mov - ing, mov - ing your feet,   back and forth now jump to the beat.   This is

ras - pa vas a bai - lar,   al de - re - cho y al re - vés.
how the dance we will do,   laugh - ing, laugh - ing all the way through.

Si quie - res tú bai - lar   la ras - pa co - mo yo,   Me
So if you want to dance   the ras - pa the way I do,   Be -

160

tie - nes que se - guir, al de - re - cho y al re - vés.
gin to move your feet, and you will be danc - ing, too.

7 / C   *Instrumental*   C   G

D₇   G   8   C   G

D₇   G   9   A

La
The

G   D₇   10

ras - pa yo bai - lé al de - re - cho y al re - vés. Si
ras - pa I will dance as for - ward and back I go. So

D₇   G

quie - res tú bai - lar, em - pie - za a mo - ver los pies.
If you want to dance, be - gin with your heel and toe.

Bogando a la luz del sol (Rowing Toward the Sunlight)

English Words by David Eddleman

Folk Song from Venezuela
Arranged by Bernie Anderson, Jr.

Flowing

So-plan las bri-sas de la_____ ma-ña-na, Ri - zan-do el la-go mur -
Soft-ly the bree-zes of morn-ing are sigh-ing, The whisp'r-ing wa-ters are

mu - ra - dor,_____ Y por o -
gent-ly stirred;_____ The sun-light

rien - te su faz a - so - ma Cual ra - ro in - cen - dio la luz del
dawn-ing from East is show-ing, Its face a - glow-ing, a rare de -

Sakura

English Version by Lorene Hoyt

Folk Song from Japan
Modern Arrangement by Henry Burnett
Arranged by S. Hagiwara

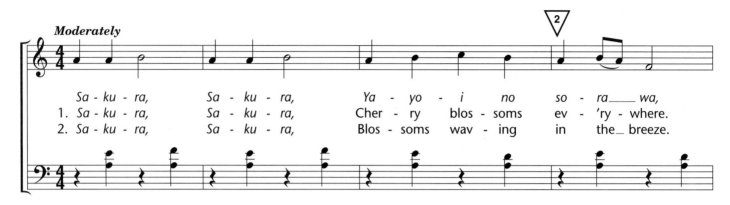

Sa - ku - ra,   Sa - ku - ra,   Ya - yo - i   no   so - ra____ wa,
1. Sa - ku - ra,   Sa - ku - ra,   Cher - ry   blos - soms   ev - 'ry - where.
2. Sa - ku - ra,   Sa - ku - ra,   Blos - soms   wav - ing   in   the__ breeze.

Mi - wa - ta - su   ka - gi - ri,   Ka - su - mi   ka   ku - mo - ka,
Clouds   of   glo - ry   fill   the__ sky,   Mist   of   beau - ty   in   the__ air,
Yo - shi - no,   the   cher - ry__ land,   Tat - su - ta,   the   ma - ple__ trees,

Ni - o - i   zo   i - zu - ru;   I - za - ya,   i - za - ya
Love - ly   col - ors   float - ing__ by,   Sa - ku - ra,   Sa - ku - ra,
Ka - ra - sa - ki,   pine   tree__ grand,   Sa - ku - ra,   Sa - ku - ra,

Mi_____ ni   yu - kan._____
Let_____ all   come__ sing - ing.
Let_____ all   come__ sing - ing.

Shri Ram, jai Ram

Hindu Chant
Arranged by Ian MacDonald

165

Feng yang hua gu (Feng Yang Song)

Folk Song from China

Steadily

VERSE

Zuo___ shou___ luo, you___ shou___ gu,
1. Sing the *Feng Yang* Song; Sing it loud and long.
2. Gifts for you have I, Kites that swoop and fly;

Shou na zhe luo___ gu lai___ chang___ ge!
Clash cym - bals, beat the drum, Strike the met - al gong!
Small trin - kets, man - y toys, All of you may buy.

Bie di___ ge er___ wo ye bu hui chang,
We are the ven - dors who trav - el all day long,
Pa - per of gold shin - ing, Bam - boo smooth and strong,

Zhi hui___ chang___ ge Feng___ Yang___ ge.
Call - ing our wares___ to the Feng - Yang - Song.
Call - ing the clear,___ ringing toy - man's song.

166

Xiao (Bamboo Flute)

Folk Song from China
Arranged by John Detroy

168

Yi di yi di xue hui liao. _____
Play a new and lilt - ing song. _____

Yibane amenu

Round from Israel
Arranged by Georgette LeNorth

Yi - ba - ne a - me - nu b - 'ar - tse - nu; B - 'ar - tse - nu,
In our land we shall re - build our na - tion. Build our na - tion

yi - ba - ne Yi - ba - ne, Yi - ba - ne, Yi - ba - ne, Yi - ba - ne.
in our land. In our land, In our land, In our land, In our land.

169

Wings of a Dove

Folk Song from the West Indies
Arranged by Don Kalbach

Since I have no wings, how can I fly?_____ Since I have no wings,

Since I have no wings, Since I have no wings, I'm gon-na sing, sing, sing, sing.

D.C. al Fine

Three Little Birds

Words and Music by Bob Marley
Arranged by Buddy Skipper

Love Can Build a Bridge

Words and Music by Paul Overstreet, Naomi Judd, and John Jarvis
Arranged by Carol Jay

174

When we stand to-geth - er,_____ it's our fin - est hour._____ We can do_____

We Shall Overcome

New Words and Arrangement by
Zilphia Horton, Frank Hamilton, Guy Carawan, and Pete Seeger

Freedom Song from the United States
Arranged by Joseph Joubert

3. We are not afraid, . . .
    We are not afraid today; . . .

4. We shall brothers be, . . .
    We shall brothers be someday; . . .

5. Truth shall make us free, . . .
    Truth shall make us free someday; . . .

Love Will Guide Us

Words by Sally Rogers

Traditional Melody
Arranged by Mark A. Miller

2. You are like no other being.
What you can give, no other can give,
To the future of our precious children.
To the future of the world where we live.
(to Refrain)

3. Hear the song of peace within you.
Heed the song of peace in your heart.
Spring's new beginning shall lead to the harvest.
Love will guide us on our way.
(to Refrain)

Big Rock Candy Mountain

Traditional
Arranged by Billy Joe Lafayette

rain does-n't fall and the wind does-n't blow, In the Big Rock Can - dy Moun-tain.
paddle all a-round in a big ca - noe, In the Big Rock Can - dy Moun-tain.

6 REFRAIN

Oh, the buzz - in' of the bees in the syc - a - more trees 'Round the

so - da wa - ter foun - tain, Where the lem - on - ade springs and the

blue - bird sings in the Big Rock Can - dy Moun - tain.

Sailing Down My Golden River

Words and Music by Pete Seeger
Arranged by Neil Swanson

1. Sail - ing down my gol - den riv - er,— Sun and wa - ter—
2. Sun and wa - ter, old life giv - ers,— I'll have them where -
3. Sun-light glanc - ing on the wa - ter,— Life and death are—
4. Life to raise my sons and daugh - ters,— Gold - en spar - kles—

all my own, And I was nev - er a - lone.
'ere I roam, And I was not far from home.
all my own, And I was nev - er a - lone.
in the foam, And I was not far from home.

Niu lang zhi nü *(The Cowherd and the Weaving Maid)*

English Words by Mary Shamrock

Folk Song from China
Arranged by Ting Ho

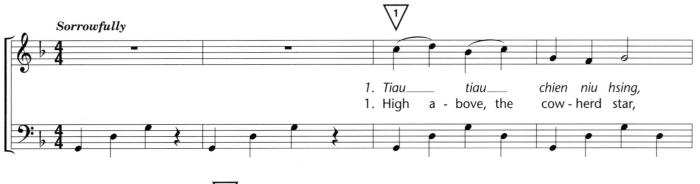

Sorrowfully

1. Tiau___ tiau___ chien niu hsing,
1. High a - bove, the cow - herd star,

jiau___ jiau___ hě han nü hsien___ hsien ien su shou
weav - ing maid, so bright, so far. Grace - ful hands, soft and white,

zha zha nong ji zhu ing ing
weav - ing through each night. Shin - ing

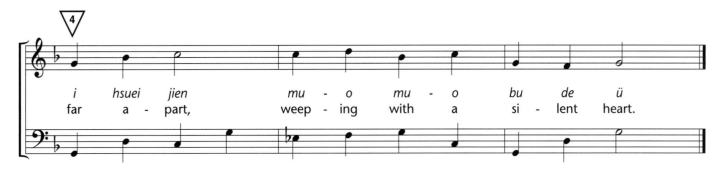

i hsuei jien mu - o mu - o bu de ü
far a - part, weep - ing with a si - lent heart.

2. Zhong zhru bu cheng zhang,
chi ti lei zhru ü
ne han ching chie chien
hsiang chü fu ji hsü
ing ing i hsuei jien
muo muo bu de ü

2. They must wait throughout the day
for the moon to light the way.
Each alone, through the years
freely flow the tears.
Shining far apart,
weeping with a silent heart.

My Bonnie Lies Over the Ocean

Folk Song from the United States
Arranged by Neil Swanson

Clementine

Folk Song from the United States
Arranged by W. W. Schmidt

1. In a cavern by a canyon, Excavating for a mine,
Dwelt a miner, forty-niner, And his daughter, Clementine.

2. Light she was and like a feather, And her shoes were number nine,
Herring boxes without topses, Sandals were for Clementine.

REFRAIN
Oh, my darlin', oh, my darlin', Oh, my darlin' Clementine,
You are lost and gone forever, Dreadful sorry, Clementine.

3. Drove she ducklings to the water
Every morning just at nine;
Struck her foot against a splinter,
Fell into the foaming brine. *Refrain*

4. Rosy lips above the water
Blowing bubbles mighty fine;
But, alas! I was no swimmer,
So I lost my Clementine. *Refrain*

Johnny Appleseed

From Rosemary and Stephen Vincent Benét

From an American Folk Hymn
in the Virginia Sacred Musical Repository

rud - dy and sound as a good ap - ple tree.
car - ried his seeds in the best deer - skin bags. John - ny
has his_ apple trees_ best still in_ bloom.

Ap - ple - seed! John - ny Ap - ple - seed!

Student Page 348

Peace Round

Traditional
Arranged by Neil Swanson

Slowly, Solemnly

What a good - ly thing, if the chil - dren of the world

could live to - geth - er in_ peace.

Somos el barco (We Are the Boat)

Words and Music by Lorre Wyatt
Arranged by Anita P. Davis

built by ma - ny___ hands.
face the wind once - more.
yet we're sail - ing___ still.

The sea we are sail - ing on___
With our hearts___ we chart the wa - ters___
With a song to help us pull to - geth - er___

D.S. al Coda ⊕ *Coda*

touch-es ev - 'ry sand.___
ne-ver sailed be - fore.___
if we on - ly will.___

So - mos el me.

This Pretty Planet

Words and Music by John Forster and Tom Chapin
Arranged by Mary Jean Nelson

For the Beauty of the Earth

Words by Folliott S. Pierpoint

Music by Conrad Kocher

1. For the beauty of the earth, For the beauty of the skies,
2. For the beauty of each hour Of the day and of the night,

For the love which from our birth, Over and around us lies.
Hill and vale and tree and flower, Sun and moon and stars of light.

Lord of all, to Thee we raise This our hymn of grateful praise.
Lord of all, to Thee we raise This our hymn of grateful praise.

3. For the joy of ear and eye,
   For the heart and mind's delight,
   For the mystic harmony
   Linking sense to sound and sight.
   Lord of all, to Thee we raise
   This our hymn of grateful praise.

4. For the joy of human love,
   Brother, sister, parent, child,
   Friends on earth and friends above,
   For all gentle thoughts and mild.
   Lord of all, to Thee we raise
   This our hymn of grateful praise.

Singin' in the Rain

Words by Arthur Freed

Music by Nacio Herb Brown
Arrangement by Cheryl Terhune Cronk

I'm sing - in' in the rain, just sing - in' in the rain. What a glo - ri-ous feel - ing, I'm hap - py a - gain! I'm laugh - ing at clouds so dark up a - bove. The sun's in my heart and I'm

ready for love. Let the storm - y clouds chase ev - 'ry - one____ from the

place. Come on____ with the rain, I've a smile____ on my face! I'll

walk down the lane with a hap - py re - frain and

sing - in',____ just sing - in' in____ the rain!

195

The Wheel of the Water

Words and Music by John Forster and Tom Chapin
Arranged by Don Kalbach

Cycle Song of Life   *(The River Song)*

Words and music by James Durst
Arranged by Neil Swanson

with her to her death be-yond e-ter-ni-ty.
know deep in his heart that there's no oth-er way.
nev-er hear the cy-cle song of life at all.

REFRAIN
Descant last time only

The riv-er just keeps flow-in' on and
And the riv-er just keeps flow-in' on and on. The

on. The sun keeps go-in' 'round
sun keeps go-in' 'round to bring the dawn. And

Starlight, Star Bright

Words and Music by James Durst
Arranged by Mary Jean Nelson

dark of night; that we might walk in truth and light.
souls, and minds; that they might bless this world in kind.
sky, and sea; and all that share life's mys - ter - y.
hope - ful prayer; for peace to flour - ish ev - 'ry-where.

Student Page 374

Sailboat in the Sky

English Words by Aura Kontra

Folk Song from Korea
Arranged by John Detroy

Smoothly

Pu reun ha nul eun - ha su ha yan jjok bae
See the small white boat in the sky, sail - ing toward the

ae, Gae su na mu han - na mu
west, High a - bove the cin - na - mon tree

to kki han ma ri, Dot dae do ah
where a rab - bit rests. With no sails or

ni dal go sat dae do up si, Ga gi do
oars, it skims o'er the Mil - ky Way, Float - ing a -

jal do gahn da so - jjok na ra ro.
mong the clouds as slow - ly it fades a - way.

Student Page 378

Shake the Papaya Down

Calypso Song
Arranged by Ruth E. Dwyer and Judith M. Waller
Edited by Henry H. Leck
Piano Arrangement by John Girt

Exuberantly

mf
F *unison*

Ma - ma says no play;
Sweet, sweet pa - pa - ya,

Shake the pa - pa - ya down. Shake the pa - pa - ya

Shake the pa - pa - ya down. Shake the pa - pa - ya

Shake the pa - pa - ya down. Shake the pa - pa - ya

down.

down.

down.

Seagull, Seagull, Sit on the Shore

Traditional
Arranged by Susan Brumfield

Cap - tain, cap - tain, hoist up the sails, hoist up the sails,

hoist up the sails. Cap - tain, cap - tain, hoist up the sails, and

sail on, my San - ty An - na.

For my love is far a - way, far a - way,

far a - way, For my love is far a - way,

Blue hor - i - zon, head-ing for home, oh, sail on, my San - ty

'Cross the waves and back a - gain, San - ty

An - na. Sail on, my

An - na. San -

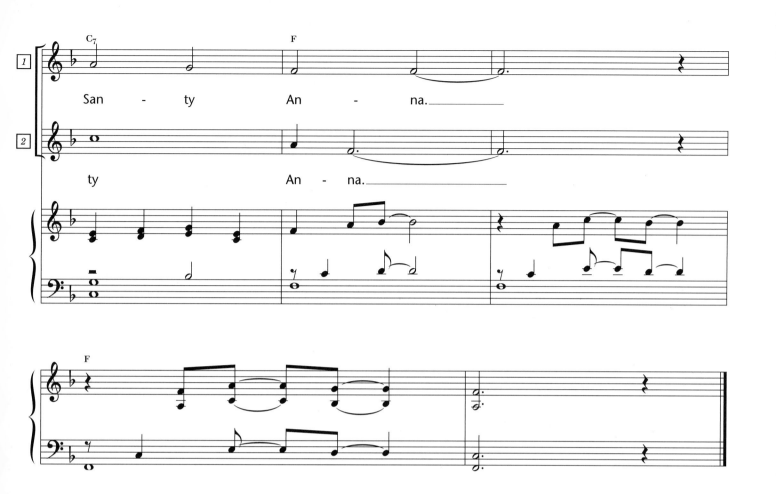

San - ty An - na.

ty An - na.

Cindy

Folk Song from the Southern United States
Arranged by Audrey Schultz

1. I wish I was an ap-ple, A-hang-in' on a tree; And ev-'ry time my
2. She took me to her par-lor, She cooled me with her fan, She swore I was the
3. Now Cin-dy is a pretty girl, Cin-dy is a peach; She threw her arms a-

Cin-dy passed She'd take a bite of me. You ought to see my Cin-dy, She
pur-tiest thing in the shape of mor-tal man. I wish I had a nee-dle, As
round my neck and hung on like a leech. Well, Cin-dy had one blue eye, She

lives a-way down South; She is so sweet the hon-ey bees All swarm a-round her
fine as I could sew, I'd sew that gal to my coat-tail, And down the road I'd
al-so had one brown; One eye looked in the coun-try, The other one looked in

Lullaby and Dance

Traditional
Arranged by Ruth E. Dwyer
Piano Arrangement by Carol Jay

218

Come out to-night, Come out to-night, Come out to - night.

Come out to-night, Come out to - night, Come out to - night.

Al - a - bam - a Gal, won't you come out to-night, Come out to-night,

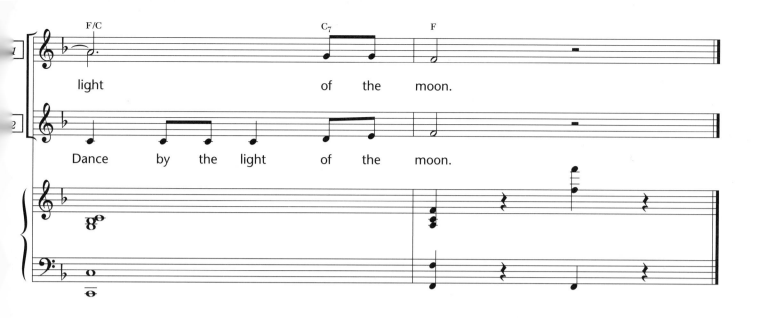

light of the moon.

Dance by the light of the moon.

Einini

Gaelic Folk Song
Arranged by Cyndee Giebler
Piano Arrangment by Carol Jay

Ein - in - i, ein -

in - i, cod - al - ai - gi, cod - al - ai - gi, ein - in - i, ein - in - i, cod - al -

Little David, Play on Your Harp

African American Spiritual
Arranged by Linda Williams

227

Sambalele

English Words by Henry Leck

Folk Song from Brazil
Vocal Arrangement by Henry Leck
Piano Accompaniment by Carlos Gonçalves

Sam-ba - le-le ta do-en - te, tac-oa ca be - ça que bra - da,
Sam-ba - le-le is a fel - low, Who rare - ly gets to his pil - low,

Sam - ba - le-le pre-ci-sa - va de u-mas de zoi - to lam-ba - das, Sam-
He spends his time loud-ly play - ing. No one can tell where he's stay - ing, Sam-

la - io meu bem, ba - la - io sin - ha, ba - la - io do co - ra - ção, Mo -
la - io, so sweet ba - la - io so kind, ba - la - io we can't ig - nore. The

ça - que não tem ba - la - io sin - ha bo - taa cos - tu - ra no
beau - ty you bring how hap - py you sing we all want to see you

chão. Ba - la - io meu bem, Ba - la - io sin - ha, ba - la - io do co - ra -
more. Ba - la - io so nice, ba - la - io pre - cise, ba - la - io you live next

chão. Sam - ba - le - le ta do - en - te, tac - oa ca - be - ça que
more. Sam - ba - le - le is a fel - low, Who rare - ly gets to his

Circle 'Round the Moon *from "Reflections of Youth"*

Words and Music by Mark Hierholzer

Cir - cle 'round the moon in - vites me to stay out in the win - ter - time.

Cry - tals in the air sug - gest that I pre - pare for the

cold night air. High a - bove the trees

you will make me see that with such a sight sheer de-light is

hid-den ev'-ry-where for those who care to see.

Cav-erns down be-low in-vite me to come down on the

slip-p'ry rock. I-ci-cles of stone and

mak - ing me long for you._____

Student Page 411

A Merry Modal Christmas

Words and Music by Bernard de la Monnoye (Pat-a-pan)
Carols from France and England
Arranged by Buryl Red

Spirited *Pat-a-pan*   *mp*   *mf*

Prum, pum, pum!   Prum, pum, pum!   *Guil - lo,*
                                       Wil - lie,

mp

Prum, pum, pum!   Prum, pum, pum!

240

prends ton tam-bou - rin, Toi prends ta flú - te, Ro - bin; Au son
get your lit - tle drum, Ro-bin, bring your flute, and come. Aren't they

Prum, pum, pum! Prum, pum, pum!

de cés in - stru - ments, Tu - re - lu - re - lu, pat - a - pat - a - pan; Au son
fun to play up on? Tu - re - lu - re - lu, pat - a - pat - a - pan; When you

Prum, pum, pum! Prum, pum, pum!

de cés in - stru - ments, Je di - rai No - ël gaie - ment.
play your fife and drum, How can an - y - one be glum?

Prum, pum, pum! Prum, pum, pum!

en - voy - a - ge___ Ce ma - tin, j'ai ren - con-tré le train, De
rid - ing proud - ly,___ This great day, I met u-pon the way, The

trois grands rois des-sus le grand che - min. Tout char - gés d'or les sui-
Kings of East with all their fine ar - ray. The gifts of gold, frank-in-

vant d'a - bord, De grands guer - riers et les gar - des du tré - sor, Tout
cense, and myrrh, Were guard - ed close by a band of stur - dy war - riors, Their

Ce ma - tin, j'ai ren - con - tré le train, De
This great day, I met up on the way, The

a - ge,___ Ce ma - tin, j'ai ren - con - tré le
proud - ly,___ This great day, I met up on the

trois grands rois des - sus le grand che - min.
Kings of East with all their grand fine ar - ray.

train, De trois grands rois des - sus le grand che -
way, The Kings of East with all their fine ar -

Ce ma - tin,   Ce ma - tin,   Ce ma - tin, ma - tin!_____
This great day,   This great day,   This great day, great   day!_____

min.   Ce ma - tin,   Ce ma - tin,   Ce ma - tin!_____
ray.   This great   day,   This great   day,   This great   day!_____

La copa de la vida (The Cup of Life)

Words and Music by Desmond Child and Robi Rosa
Arranged by Buddy Skipper

251

Shir l'shalom (Hand in Hand — A Song for Peace)

Hebrew Words by Jacob Rotblitt
English Adaptation by Stanley Ralph Ross and Michael Isaacson

Music by Yair Rosenblum
Arranged by David Eddleman

ni - tsa - chon___ v' - lo shi - rey ha - lel.
ki - ka - rot___ ha - ri - u l' - sha - lom!   La' chen rak
all a - live,___ is God's e - ter - nal___ love. And so we
war is banned___ and peace will con - quer___ fear.

shi - ru   shir l' - sha - lom,___   al til - cha - shu tfi -
sing,   sing,   sing of a day___   when peace will reign su -

la.   La' chen rak shi - ru   shir l' - sha - lom,___   bi -
preme;   And so we sing,   sing,   sing and we pray___   that

Little Shop of Horrors

Words by Howard Ashman

Music by Alan Menken
Arranged by Buddy Skipper

258

Shang-a-lang, feel the *Sturm* and *Drang* in the air.

(Yeah,_ yeah,_ yeah.)_____ Sha-la-la, stop right where you are. Don't

move a thing.__ You bet-ter, you bet-ter,

tell-in' you, you bet-ter tell your ma-ma

Winter Fantasy

Words and Music by Jill Gallina
Arranged by Don Kalbach

263

Let It Snow! Let It Snow! Let It Snow!

Word by Sammy Cahn

Music by Jule Styne
Arranged by John Girt

When we fi-nal-ly kiss good-night, how I'll hate go-ing out in the storm! But if

you'll real-ly hold me tight, all the way home I'll be warm. The

fire is slow-ly dy-ing, and, my dear, we're still good-bye-ing. But as

long as you love me so, Let it snow! Let it snow! Let it snow!

Ocho kandelikas (Eight Little Candles)

Words and Music by Flory Jagoda
Arranged by Ting Ho

kuat-ro kan-de-li - kas, sin-ko kan-de-li - kas, sej kan-de-li - kas,

four_ lit - tle can - dles, five_ lit - tle can - dles, six lit - tle can - dles,

sie - te kan-de-li - kas, o - cho kan-de-las pa - ra mi.

sev - en lit - tle can - dles, eight lit - tle can-dles all for me.

3. *Los pastelikos vo komer*
kon almendrikas i la myel.
Los pastelikos vo komer
kon almendrikas i la myel.
Refrain

3. Sweet little pastries we will eat,
filled with almonds and honey.
Sweet little pastries we will eat,
filled with almonds and honey.
Refrain

The Twelve Days of Christmas

Christmas Song from England
Arranged by James Harris

268

6. On the sixth   day   of Christ - mas   my   true love gave to   me (go to 7,6) etc.
(seventh, eighth, ninth, tenth, eleventh, twelfth)

12. TWELFTH DAY   *11. ELEVENTH DAY*   *10. TENTH DAY*

Twelve   drum - mers drum - ming;   Eleven   pip - ers pip - ing;   Ten   lords a - leap - ing;

9. NINTH DAY   *8. EIGHTH DAY*   *7. SEVENTH DAY*

Nine   la - dies danc - ing;   Eight   maids a - milk - ing;   Seven   swans a swim - ming;

Six geese a - lay-ing; Five gold - en rings; Four__ call-ing birds;

Three French hens; Two__ tur - tle doves and a par - tridge__ in a pear tree.

Al quebrar la piñata (Piñata Song)

English Words by Verne Muñoz

Christmas Song from Mexico
Arranged by Rosemary Jacques

En las no - ches de po - sa - das,_____ La pi - ña - ta es
In the hap - py days of Christ - mas,_____ Sounds of glad - ness

lo me - jor;_____ La ni - ña más re - mil -
fill the air;_____ When it's time for the pi -

ga - da_____ Se al - bo - ro - ta con ar - dor._____
ña - ta,_____ There's ex - cite - ment ev - 'ry - where._____

Harambee

Words and Music by James McBride
Arranged by Joseph Joubert

Sharing in a peaceful time of trust and love and song,— With
Hoping that the best__ of all your wish-es do come true,— We
Caring is a part__ of our re-spon-si-bil-i-ty.__ We

joy e-nough to last__ the whole year long.
wish a hap-py Kwan-zaa to you.
want the world to live__ in har-mo-ny.

Kwan-zaa hol-i-day____ is a spe-cial hol-i-day,____ A

*ram - bee*____ *means*____ *hel - lo and good - bye, too,*____ A

time to cel - e - brate____ our his - to - ry.   Ha -

way of show - ing that____ I care for you.

(Last time only)

to next verse

We Shall Not Be Moved

Traditional Freedom Song
Arranged by Alice Firgau

1. We shall not, we shall not be
2. We're on our way to vic-tor - y,___ we shall not be
3. Segre - ga-tion is___ our en - e - my, it must be re -

moved.___ We shall not, we shall not be
moved.___ We're on our way to vic-tor - y,___ we shall not be
moved.___ Segre - ga-tion is___ our en - e - my,___ it must be re -

moved.
moved. Just like a tree, that's plant - ed by the wa -
moved.

ter, We shall not be moved.

277

Dayenu (It Would Have Been Enough)

Jewish Passover Song
Arranged by David ben Avraham

3. *Ilu natan natan lanu,*
natan lanu et haTora,
natan lanu et haTora, dayenu.
Refrain

3. Had he given us the Tora,
only given us the Tora,
Had he given us the Tora, *dayenu.*
Refrain

America

Words by Samuel Francis Smith

Traditional Melody

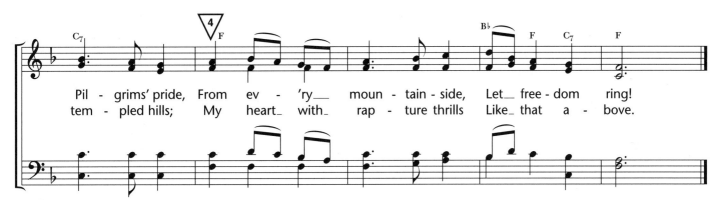

1. My country! 'tis of thee, Sweet land of liberty, Of thee I sing; Land where my fathers died, Land of the Pilgrims' pride, From ev'ry mountain-side, Let freedom ring!

2. My native country, thee, Land of the noble free, Thy name I love; I love thy rocks and rills, Thy woods and templed hills; My heart with rapture thrills Like that above.

3. Let music swell the breeze,
   And ring from all the trees
   Sweet Freedom's song;
   Let mortal tongues awake,
   Let all that breathe partake,
   Let rocks their silence break,
   The sound prolong.

4. Our fathers' God, to Thee,
   Author of liberty,
   To Thee we sing;
   Long may our land be bright
   With Freedom's holy light;
   Protect us by Thy might,
   Great God, our King!

The Star-Spangled Banner

Words by Francis Scott Key

Music by John Stafford Smith

CREDITS AND ACKNOWLEDGMENTS

CREDITS AND ACKNOWLEDGMENTS *continued*

SONG INDEX

SONG INDEX *continued*

NOTE: These page numbers refer to the actual page in this book. Page numbers for the Pupil Edition appear above the title of each arrangement.